Capital Requirements Directive and Spiral Death in the Financial Market

by

Beatriz McCarron

Illustrations by Ingram Pinn

ISBN: 978-0-9535537-4-7

To my children Hannah and Jamie.

I dedicate this book to the memory of my parents

Celina Marrugo de Gamez and Hernando Gamez Roa,

Co-founders of Colombian Radio Station La Voz de Garagoa.

CONTENTS

ACKNOWLEDGMENTS

Thanks to Professor Dr. Joseph Tanega for his supervision and invaluable contribution.

I am highly indebted and grateful to Mr Ingram Pinn, Financial Times illustrator for his permission to reproduce the four illustrations related to the Credit Crunch. I offer my sincere admiration for his work.

Many thanks to Mr Richard Pidgen, Syndication Rights & Operations Manager of the Financial Times Permissions and Reprints Department for helping me to get permission to reprint Ingram Pinn's illustrations.

Thanks to Peter McCarron for his helpful advice and proofreading.

My appreciation to Margaret and Ernest Hird for their encouragement and support.

Also I wish to express my gratitude to Mike Pilley for his advice and graphic design suggestions.

ABBREVIATIONS

AAA	Meaning: Highest Credit Quality
CRD	Capital Requirements Directive
EC	European Community
ECJ	European Court of Justice
EU	European Union
FASB	Financial Accounting Standard Board
FSA	Financial Services Authority
IAS	International Accounting Standard
IASB	International Accounting Standard Board
IFRS	International Financial Reporting Standards
MBS	Mortgage Backed Securities
MS	Member State
MSs	Member States
NRV	Net Realisable Value

A NOTE BY THE AUTHOR

This work first appeared as a dissertation and it was timely because it coincided with the Credit Crunch of 2008.

At the time this book was published the disintegration of the European Community started with the United Kingdom post-referendum: Brexit and other European countries possibly trying to follow UK's lead.

I have been given permission to reprint four illustrations made by Ingram Pinn, Financial Times illustrator, which were published by the Financial Times at the time of the Credit Crunch.

EU BAIL-OUT   *Ingram Pinn*   1

This illustration well captured the financial despair, the market downward spiral and envisaged the collapse of the European Union.

---

[1] Ingram Pinn illustration available at http://search.ft.com, accessed 17th October 2008

INTRODUCTION

The chaos of the financial system has plumbed new depths with the failure of Bear Stearns, the fifth largest investment bank in the US, now commentators fear the entire banking system is on the brink of a 1930s[2] style collapse. Wild fluctuations within the stock markets[3] is just one indication of a global economy that is out of control – and every "solution" put forward serves only to temporarily

---

[2] Koo, R. (2008) "Insight: Japan's lessons could ease crisis", *Financial Times*, 2008, available at http://search.ft.com accessed 5th April 2008.

[3] See Bouchaud, J, Gefen, Y, Potters, M, Wyart, M. (2003) "Fluctuations and response in financial markets: the subtle nature of 'random' price changes", at SSRN: http://papers.ssrn.com accessed 5th April 2008.

resolve one problem by creating another.

Alan Greenspan, the former head of the US Federal Reserve Bank, wrote in the Financial Times recently, "The current financial crisis in the US is likely to be judged in retrospect as the most wrenching since the end of the Second World War".[4] In February 2008 when New York economist Nouriel Roubini suggested $1,000-2,000 billion losses in the financial sector alone, he was ridiculed by mainstream commentators.[5] Today those same commentators are running to catch up with Roubini, and he, in turn, has revised his estimate upwards.

Prof. Roubini talks of a $5,600 billion (£2,773 billion) decline in the value of stocks and the possibility of additional trillions of dollars in losses on commercial property. Total losses might even equal annual GDP.[6]

---

[4] Greenspan, A. (2008) "We will never have a perfect model of risk", Financial Times at http://search.ft.com accessed 25 March 2008.

[5] Martin Wolf, M. (2008) "Going, going, gone: a rising auction of scary scenarios", Financial Times at http://search.ft.com accessed 25 March 2008.

[6] Id.

Main Research Question

This analysis endeavours to answer the question: whether the Capital Requirements Directive (CRD) is going to enforce 'spiral death' in the financial market.

In the course of answering this question the first issue to be discussed is the Directive's 'fair value rule'[7] and how it can impact the performance of financial institutions. Secondly will be addressed the 'prudential supervision system'[8] relating to the financial crisis.

These aspects are prerequisites for an understanding of significant issues concerning the implementation of the CRD and the possibility that its implementation may trigger a 'death spiral' in the credit market, a question that finally will be summarized in the conclusion.

---

[7] Directive 2006/48/EC of 14 June 2006 relating to the taking up and pursuit of the business of credit institutions (recast), Title V, Chapter 2, Section 1, Article 64 (4).

[8] Ibid. Title V, Chapter 1, Section 1, Article 40.

Objective

To examine whether or not the implementation of the new regulatory framework (CRD) will adversely affect financial institutions under actual financial crunch.

1. To examine the impact of the 'fair value rule'.

2. To analyse the influence of the 'prudential supervision system'.

Market Background

This is an intriguing time for this essay to be written; considering the deterioration of conditions in the financial markets surrounded by the losses of a sub-prime crisis, the US recession, collateral values declining, the European economies slowing down, the Bank of England decreasing interest rates, and the sterling and dollar losing value against the euro.

Legislative Background

The European financial sector saw in 2007 the introduction of new regulations under the Capital Requirements Directive, this new framework emerged in the wake of the US sub-prime crisis and, inevitably, is affecting European economies in an era of globalization.

The Capital Requirements Directive amalgamated two directives of the European Parliament and of the Council: Directive 2006/48/EC relating to the taking up and pursuit of the business of credit institutions and Directive 2006/49/EC on the capital adequacy of investment firms and credit institutions; both of the 14th of June 2006. This Directive came into force on 1st of January 2007, but full implementation was expected from January 2008.

The provisions in the Capital Requirements Directive on minimum capital requirements and capital adequacy of investment firms and credit institutions are the provisions established in the Basel

II[9] framework agreement on the international convergence of capital measurement and capital requirements adopted by the Basel Committee on Banking Supervision on the 26th of June 2004.[10] Basel II is the Supervisory Review Process of the Basel Accord I 1988. The main objective of Basel II is to improve capital regulations and to develop a more risk-sensitive framework that would strengthen the stability of the international banking system, taking into account changes in banking and risk management across different countries.[11]

The revised Framework is more risk sensitive than the 1988 Accord; it introduces a higher number of risk assessments based on banks' internal systems. It also sets up the regulations to put forward the minimum requirements with a view toward enhancing transparency in these internal risk assessment

---

[9] Basel II: International Convergence of Capital Measurement and Capital Standards: A Revised Framework available at http://www.bis.org
[10] Id.
[11] Id.

processes.[12] Transparency is one of the conditions established by this Directive in order to achieve an effective platform for banking supervision and to enhance credibility between the citizens of the Union.

Basel II provides a range of options for determining the capital requirements for credit risk and operational risk, to be applied within a banking group; in other words it allows banks and supervisors to exercise some discretion in selecting the approaches according to their operations and their financial market infrastructure.[13] The Framework also allows for a limited degree of national discretion in the implementation of the different options, which will be discussed in chapter three of this paper.

Despite the fact that Basel II has been implemented through the CRD, Basel regulations are not binding within the European Community. The CRD Directive has to be implemented as national law, which must be adjusted in harmony within the

---

[12] See Directive 2006/48/EC, Title IV, Chapter 2, Section 3, Article 81.

[13] Basel II: International Convergence of Capital Measurement and Capital Standards: A Revised Framework available at http://www.bis.org

EC Treaty. The European Court of Justice (ECJ) established the concept of direct effect in the case of *Van Gend en Loos [1963]*.[14]

The rationale behind the "principle of harmonious interpretation"[15] is to ensure the common recognition of banking supervision[16] through the European realm. Enforcing this principle will reassert the supremacy of Community law through the Member States (MSs). The aim of the Directive is to introduce a prudential supervision system[17], which will provide the possibility of granting a single licence recognised across the EU financial market.

---

[14] Case 26-62 Van Gend en Loos [1963] ECR 13, the judgment of the ECJ established that art. 12 of the EU Treaty should be interpreted as 'producing direct effects and conferring individuals' rights'.

[15] Craig, P, De Búrca, G, EU Law: Text, Cases, and Materials, fourth edition (Oxford: Oxford University Press, 2008) at pp 287.

[16] See Mitchener, KJ, Are Prudential Supervision and Regulation Pillars of Financial Stability? (US, Cambridge: National Bureau of Economic Research, Inc., 2006)

[17] Directive 2006/48/EC, para. (4).

CRD Scope

Directive 2006/49/EC establishes the rules and calculation of capital adequacy requirements that apply to investment firms and credit institutions[18] for their prudential supervision.[19] The introduction of this international framework coincides with a turbulent time in the financial world, affected by the defaults on US subprime mortgages that has triggered a credit crisis.

Directive 2006/48/EC in Article 1 introduces rules concerning the taking up and pursuit of the business of credit institutions, and their prudential supervision.[20] According to article 2 this Directive does not apply to central banks of Member States and post office giro institutions.

In the United Kingdom, the CRD is not applicable to the National Savings Bank, the Commonwealth Development Finance Company Ltd, the Agricultural

---

[18] For definitions see Directive 2006/49/EC, Section 2, Article 3.

[19] Ibid., for scope see Section 2, Article 2.

[20] Ibid., Article 39 and Title V, Chapter 4, Section 1 shall apply to financial holding companies and mixed-activity holding companies which have their head offices in the Community.

Mortgage Corporation Ltd, the Scottish Agricultural Securities Corporation Ltd, the Crown Agents for overseas governments and administrations, credit unions, and municipal banks.

Requirements for the taking up and pursuit of the business of credit institutions:

- Credit institutions need to obtain authorisation from the competent authorities of the Member State before commencing their activities.[21]

- Credit institutions need to possess separate own funds.[22]

- Initial capital at time of authorisation cannot be less than 5 million euros.[23]

- There must be at least two persons who effectively direct the business of the credit institution, with sufficiently good reputation and sufficient experience to perform such duties.[24]

---

[21] Directive 2006/48/EC, Title II, Article 6.
[22] Ibid., Article 10.
[23] Ibid., Article 9.
[24] Ibid., Article 11.

- Competent authorities must be informed of "the identities of the shareholders or members, whether direct or indirect, natural or legal persons, that have qualifying holdings, and of the amounts of those holdings".[25]

- Credit institutions shall notify the Commission when an authorisation is granted, and the Commission will publish a list of institutions, which have been granted authorisation in the Official Journal of the European Union.[26]

The competent authorities may not grant or withdraw an authorisation if the above mentioned requirements are not fulfilled, or in situations where it is obvious that a credit institution has opted for the legal system of one of the Community countries in order to evade the stricter standards enforced by another Member State.[27]

---

[25] Ibid., Article 12.
[26] Ibid., Article 14.
[27] Ibid., para. (10).

Minimum Capital Requirements under Directive 2006/48/EC

The Directive establishes minimum capital requirements, which play a central role in the supervision of credit institutions and in the assessment of their main risks, such as credit risks,[28] market risks,[29] operational[30] and liquidity risks.[31] The provisions in this area should be considered in conjunction with other specific instruments and in harmony with fundamental techniques for the supervision of the Community's credit institutions.[32] In other words the Directive wants to lay down common minimum capital requirements across the European Community as a measure to ensure "adequate solvency", [33] which weighs assets and off-balance-sheet items according to the degree of risk.[34]

---

[28] Ibid., para. (43).
[29] Ibid., Annex V, para.7.
[30] Ibid., para 9.
[31] Ibid., para. (69).
[32] Ibid., para (15).
[33] Directive 2006/48/EC, para. (46).
[34] Ibid., para. (45).

The Directive determines that "the minimum capital requirements should be proportionate to the risks addressed".[35] In particular the reduction in risk levels deriving from having a large number of relatively small exposures should be reflected in the requirements.[36] According to this Directive it is necessary that risk-sensitive measures are implemented in order to ensure that the risks and risk reductions arising from credit institutions' securitisation activities and investments are appropriately monitored.

Credit institutions must be able to map their historical internal loss data into the business lines and operational risk losses that are related to market risks (exposures from all appropriate subsystems and geographic locations) should be included in the scope of the capital requirement for operational risk. Information must be available to the MS's competent authorities upon request.

---

[35] Ibid., para. (40).
[36] Id.

Minimum Capital Requirements under Directive 2006/49/EC

This Directive establishes that "in order to ensure adequate solvency of institutions within a group, it is essential that the minimum capital requirements apply on the basis of the consolidated financial situation of the group". As Directive 2006/48/EC does not apply to groups which include one or more investment firms but no credit institutions, Directive 2006/49/EC introduced in Section 2 the requirements for the supervision of investment firms on a consolidated basis.

Under Article 22 the competent authorities are responsible for exercising supervision of investment firms on a consolidated basis, and "on a case-by-case basis".[37] This supervision should include evaluation of the adequacy of own funds of institutions.[38] The own funds of investment firms or credit institutions[39] is

---

[37] Directive 2006/49/EC of 14 June 2006 on the capital adequacy of investment firms and credit institutions (recast), Chapter V, Section 2, Article 22.

[38] Ibid., para. (30).

[39] Directive 2004/39/EC does not, however, establish common

considered to be useful "to absorb losses which are not matched by a sufficient volume of profits, to ensure the continuity of institutions and to protect investors".[40]

Institutions are requested to have internal capital which is "adequate in quantity, quality and distribution"[41] in accordance with the risk exposure within a group. [42] The minimum capital requirements are applied to credit risk, market risk, and operational risk:

a.   Credit Risk

The CRD regulatory framework is primarily based on assessing the credit risk rather than liquidity risk. Credit risk is basically the risk that financial institutions carry in face of the possibility that borrowers or counterparts may fail to fulfil their payment obligations. The

---

standards for the own funds of investment firms nor indeed does it establish the amounts of the initial capital of such firms or a common framework for monitoring the risks incurred by them.

[40] Directive 2006/49/EC, para. (12).

[41] Ibid., para. (29).

[42] Ibid., para. (27).

controversial opinion about the system introduced by the Capital Requirement Directive is that it requires a more detailed pricing regime which includes other risk structures.

b.   Market Risk

Supervision of market risk is effective since the first of January 2007. The Directive calls on the competent authorities of Member States to cooperate in order to achieve a more effective supervision.[43]

A 'Margin Period of Risk' will be considered "from the last exchange of collateral covering a netting set of transactions with a defaulting counterpart until that counterpart is closed out and the resulting market risk is re-hedged".[44]

In other words, institutions not only are required to monitor their own internal position risk but also that of counterparties, as part of the credit risk calculations.

---

[43] Ibid., para. (21).
[44] Ibid., Annex II, para. 10.

c.   Operational Risk

The Directive defines 'operational risk'[45] as the risk of loss resulting from inadequate or failed internal processes, people and systems or from external events, and includes legal risk;[46] these risks include: processes, such as internal operational methods, bank reporting process; people, e.g. management failures; systems, such as IT systems; external events, such as market crash or an earthquake.

Securitisation

The Directive provides some financial definitions as well as limits in respect of large exposures. Securitisation is defined under section 4, article 36 as "a transaction or scheme, whereby the credit risk[47] associated with an exposure or pool of exposures is

---

[45] Ibid., Annex V, 9 outline Operational risk.
[46] Ibid., Title I, Article 4(22).
[47] Ibid., Annex V outlines the Securitisation Risk.

tranched,[48] having the following characteristics":[49]

- Payments in the transaction or scheme are dependent upon the performance of the exposure or pool of exposures.[50]

- The subordination of tranches determines the distribution of losses during the ongoing life of the transaction or scheme.[51]

The Directive establishes two kinds of securitisations:

- The first one is 'traditional securitisation' involving the economic transfer of the exposures being securitised to a securitisation special purpose entity which issues securities.[52]

---

[48] Ibid., Section 4, Article 39: 'tranche' means a contractually established segment of the credit risk associated with an exposure or number of exposures, where a position in the segment entails a risk of credit loss greater than or less than a position of the same amount in each other such segment, without taking account of credit protection provided by third parties directly to the holders of positions in the segment or in other segments;…

[49] Id.

[50] Id.

[51] Id.

[52] Ibid., Article 4(37).

- The second is 'synthetic securitisation' where the tranching is achieved by the use of credit derivatives or guarantees, and the pool of exposures is not removed from the balance sheet of the originator credit institution.[53]

Capital Adequacy under Directive 2006/49/EC

This Directive relating to the establishment of the capital adequacy requirements applying to investment firms and credit institutions introduces the rules for their calculation, and the rules for their prudential supervision.[54]According to Jonathan Ward, "the capital adequacy regulation provides significant opportunities for manipulation by banks and supervisors, and may itself be ineffective as a result". [55] This confirms how flexible the regulations are and suggests that perhaps the framework should impose more rigorous boundaries that might help clarify its application.

---

[53] Ibid., para. (38).
[54] See Directive 2006/49/EC, para. (5).
[55] Ward, J. (2002) "The Supervisory Approach: A critique", ESRC Centre for Business Research, pp 4.

This Directive recapitulates one of the objectives of Directive 2004/39/EC, which allow MS's investment firms authorised by the competent authorities to establish branches and provide services freely in other Member States. Accordingly, the Directive provides the rules governing the authorisation and pursuit of the business of investment firms in pursuing the aims of the Treaty, and thereby seeks to establish a harmonised market.

Annex I ratifies the position relating to the capital adequacy requirements as set out in Directive 2006/48/EC, leaving discretion for institutions to establish the liquidity and investment quality of financial instruments. The possibility that supervisors may over-rely on managerial discretion in their risk assessment process is certainly a potential weakness, given the present economic and political climate, and hardly seems conducive to market discipline.

Research Methodology

The initial research method was based on a literature review on the topic of the impact of the Capital Requirements Directive (CRD): Directive 2006/48/EC and Directive 2006/49/EC.

An outline of two regulatory frameworks: Basel II and CRD's principal aspects, was carried out to understand these regulatory frameworks in order to establish the main areas where critiques can be made in light of the present credit crisis.

Structure

The study will be divided into three main chapters. The first chapter introduces the purpose of the new regulatory framework and how the analysis will be conducted in order to reach the answer to the problem question. The justification forms part of this introductory chapter.

The second chapter will discuss how the implementation of the fair value rule introduced by the CRD may affect the credit grading of financial institutions under current market conditions. This chapter will also consider some objections to IAS 39 rules.

The third chapter will discuss, in the light of present economic conditions, whether or not the new rules and calculations for the prudential supervision system might improve the monitoring of risks taken by credit institutions. The argument will counterpose the concept of transparency versus discretion.

CAPITAL REQUIREMENTS DIRECTIVE AND ITS FAIR VALUE RULE

According to regulations defined by the Capital Requirements Directive, "institutions shall establish and maintain systems and controls sufficient to provide prudent and reliable valuation estimates".[56] Compliance with these rules means that the value applied to trading books will reflect the current market value, which in substance seems to be "the

---

[56] To expand see Directive 2006/49/EC, Annex VII, Part B.

same as fair value".[57] The most common use of the fair value concept "is probably in acquisition accounting, where separable assets and liabilities are measured at fair value at the end of the acquisition".[58]

Current disclosure requirements measure the value of assets and liabilities on different levels. "Credit institutions shall not include in own funds either the fair value reserves related to gains or losses on cash flow hedges of financial instruments measured at amortised cost, or any gains or losses on their liabilities valued at fair value that are due to changes in the credit institutions' own credit standing".[59] Accordingly financial institutions are required to assess the fair value of assets and only measure liabilities at amortised cost.

---

[57] The Institute of Chartered Accountants, Fair Value Accounting available at www.icaew.co.uk
[58] Id.
[59] Directive 2006/49/EC, Annex VII, Part B, Chapter 2, Section 1, Article 64 (4).

Fear of Fair Value

The UK's Financial Accounting Standards Board (FASB) defines "fair value[60] as the price that would be received to sell an asset or paid to transfer a liability in an orderly transaction between market participants at the measurement date".[61] In the process of selling financial assets, the fair value assessment will result in an "exchange price"[62] which reflects contemporary market economic conditions at the measurement date.

---

[60] The Finance Act 1998 defines 'Fair Value' in section 85(1), in relation to any loan relationship of a company, means the amount which, at the time as at which the value falls to be determined, is the amount that the company would obtain from or, as the case may be, would have to pay to an independent person for: (1) the transfer of the company's rights under the relationship in respect of amounts which at that time are not yet due and payable; and (2) the release of all the company's liabilities under the relationship in respect of amounts which at that time are not yet due and payable: pp 85(6), 86(7), 90(7). 'Independent person' means a knowledgeable and willing party dealing at arm's length: s 103(1).

[61] Financial Standards Accounting Board, Fair Value Measurement Project June 28, 2006 at http://72.3.243.42/board_handouts/06-28-06.pdf, accessed 5th March 2008.

[62] See Landsman, W. (2006) "Fair value accounting for financial instruments: some implications for bank regulation", Monetary and Economic Department, available at http://www.bis.org/publ/work209.pdf, accessed 28th January 2008.

In 2005 the European Commission decided that all listed companies should follow the International Financial Reporting Standards (IFRS)[63] published by the International Accounting Standards Board (IASB), which introduced an option of 'fair value' of financial assets in the version of IAS 39[64], and which defines fair value as the "amount for which an asset could be exchanged, or a liability settled, between knowledgeable, willing parties in an arm's length transaction".[65]

Since IAS 39 establishes rules to measure financial instruments in four measurement categories – "financial instruments at fair value through profit or loss, held-to-maturity investments, available-for-sale financial assets, and loans and receivables"[66] – these categories can be very difficult to understand and this is a manifest disadvantage in the application and

---

[63] The EU two years after the adoption of IFRS, Insight, Q4, 2007, p.4 at www.iasb.org, accessed on 7 March 2008.

[64] IAS 39 follows the US accounting rules.

[65] 22070. IAS 39: Determination of fair value, Inland Revenue Manuals, 2005, at http://www.lexisnexis.com, accessed 12 March 2008.

[66] Extract from the IASB discussion paper (for comments only) at www.iasb.org accessed 21 March 2008.

elaboration of financial reports, which as a result may not cope with the dynamism of the actual financial environment.

Sir David Tweedie, chairman of the International Accounting Standards Board, considers that IAS 39 has become "well-nigh incomprehensible".[67] This standard regulation is based on complex accounting of financial instruments, and the "poor understanding of the risks involved in complex financial instruments" [68] can be considered one of the elements that have fuelled the current financial-solvency crisis. In other words, financial institutions have been expanding and undertaking considerable amounts of risk without a proper understanding not only of the financial consequences should such transactions fail but also the regulations that apply to those transactions. It is paradoxical that while IAS 39 regulations were introduced with the aim of increasing the levels of credibility and transparency in the Member States'

---

[67] Tweedie, D. (2008) "Solutions now sought to add transparency", Financial Times, pp 26.
[68] Ibid., this idea is based on the arguments of Sir David Tweedie, chairman of the International Accounting Standards Board.

financial markets, instead they are having the opposite effect in that they are breeding an atmosphere of mistrust and confusion between financial institutions and users of financial statements, as it seems that no one knows with certainty how to apply these new rules due to their "complexity".[69]

According to the discussion paper on "Reducing Complexity in Reporting Financial Instruments",[70] published by the IASB, complexity is considered one of the most important aspects in "financial reporting", [71] and financial instruments are regarded as one of the "most complex things on which to report clearly".[72] The lack of clarity in financial reporting has probably been aggravated by "financial deregulation",[73] which

---

[69] Id.

[70] The IASB Discussion Paper is for comment only and can be accessed at www.iasb.org

[71] Id.

[72] Id. A draft decision memorandum published in January 2008 by the Advisory Committee on Improvements to Financial Reporting (chartered by the US Securities and Exchange Commission) defines complexity as the state of being difficult to understand and apply, and refers primarily to the difficulty for users to understand the economic substance of a transaction or event and the overall financial position and results of the company,...

[73] Vidal, G, Correa, E. (1996) "Deregulation and Risks in

permitted the adoption of practices that may diminish the supervision process, and hence make it very difficult for governments to prevent the eruption of actual financial crisis.

Another issue discussed in the IASB paper is that all financial instruments should be measured in the same way in order to "make the reported information easier to understand and facilitate comparisons between entities and between periods";[74] but it could be argued that a problem may arise if all the financial instruments are valued under the same general principles without taking into account the different market and instruments' characteristics, as could be the case for valuing illiquid instruments, which has proven to be particularly problematic for the financial sector.

Financial Markets," at http://papers.ssrn.com, accessed 5th April 2008.

[74] The IASB Discussion Paper is for comment only and can be accessed at www.iasb.org

Fair Value Of Assets

IAS 39 specifies "that when an active market exists where quotes are available for the asset, the appropriate measure of fair value is its current bid price (exit value)".[75] According to this rule it is relatively straightforward to use an instrument's selling value "when fair value is well defined, but is somewhat arbitrary when it is not".[76] Problems can arise for example when a market doesn't exist, or in the valuation of illiquid instruments, and there is room for the management to estimate a value that may not correspond to the accurate market situation.

But when a market is not active, according to IAS 39, "fair value is to be established by using a valuation technique

---

[75] Peasnell, K. (2006) "Institution-specific value", Monetary and Economic Department, No. 210.
[76] To expand see Jopson, B. (2007) "UK Accountants hit out at 'fair value' rules", Financial Times, available at http://www.ft.com/home/uk, accessed 11th November 2007.

... [that] (a) incorporates all factors that market participants would consider in setting a price and (b) is consistent with accepted economic methodologies for pricing financial instruments.[77]

With different valuation techniques that include options to adopt pricing models it will be difficult to establish the difference between "the institution-specific value and the ideal of an arms-length market value".[78] Fair value has become "unpopular when applied to non-traded"[79] financial instruments. Absence of a market may alone explain a lack of clarity in the fair value process, a problem exacerbated by allowing the use of subjective judgement on the part of management in the overall valuation process.

In light of accounting principles, an asset's value based on market value "should not be carried on a

---

[77] Paragraphs AG74 and AG76 as cited in Peasnell, K, (2006) "Institution-specific value", Monetary and Economic Department, No. 210.
[78] Id.
[79] See Jopson, B. (2007) "UK Accountants hit out at 'fair value' rules", Financial Times, available at http://www.ft.com/home/uk, accessed 11th November 2007.

balance sheet at more than its recoverable amount".[80] The implications are that if an asset is included in the balance sheet for a certain amount that asset could be sold for that amount, or it could generate cash flows in present value terms.

Recoverable amount is the higher of:[81]

- Net realisable value (NRV) (IFRS term: fair value less costs to sell); and

- Value in use

Table 1[82]

Fixed assets	Current assets
Tangible assets	Cash
Intangible assets	Investments
Investments	Debtors

---

[80] To expand this concept see Holgate, P, Accounting for Lawyers (Cambridge: Cambridge University Press, 2006) p.119.
[81] Id.
[82] Id.

Fair Value of Liabilities

According to the ASB's principles, liabilities are defined as an "obligation of an entity to transfer economic benefits as a result of past transactions or events". [83] Under this statement liabilities are considered an 'obligation', [84] which can be generated from "deposits in a bank or loans granted to customers".[85] Of course, fluctuations in interest rates can instantly affect the fair value of these liabilities in either direction.[86]

The potential exposure of liabilities under the new CRD framework can reduce credit standards and negatively affect financial institutions. Some academics agree that "liabilities should be measured at the best estimate of the amount that will be required to settle

---

[83] Id. pp 123.
[84] Id. To expand this idea see "Approaches to addressing measurement and related problems"
[85] Peasnell, K. (2006) "Institution-specific value", Monetary and Economic Department, No. 210.
[86] Id.

them".[87] The credit crisis is exposing potential liabilities, just recently a complaint has been filed in New York by the financial Guaranty Insurance Company (bond insurer) accusing the German Bank IKB and its affiliates of a fraud that left it exposed to potential liabilities of $1.9bn.[88] This case is grist to the mill for those critics who argue that the structure of the credit market is not functioning properly.

CRD and IAS 39 Issues

The European Commission has "reflected a strong political commitment to endorse the standards issued by the IASB".[89] IAS 39 changed the accounting practice based on historical cost towards the valuation of assets and liabilities at fair value. For investments and other financial institutions, valuation of assets depends on the rules established by four categories

---

[87] Id. pp 125.

[88] Duyn, A, Wilson, J, (2008) "FGIC sues IKB over $1.9bn liabilities", Financial Times at http://www.ft.com/home/uk

[89] Staff team led by Enria, A. (2004) "Fair Value Accounting and Financial Stability", Occasional Paper No.13.

under IAS 39 while the measurement of intangibles is usually carried out on a cost basis.[90]

As Professor Bert Bruggink (2003) notes, one of the main objections to IAS 39 rules is the fact that its provisions are one-sided. "In other words: a number of instruments on the asset side of the balance sheet are automatically subject to marking to market".[91] Marking to market financial instruments – which came into widespread use in the 1990s – can result in a high degree of "volatility"[92] of earnings and/or "shareholders' equity".[93]

A recent example is the case of "MBIA, the monoline insurer, where marking financial instruments to market threw up a pre-tax loss of $3.5bn". [94] This is a paradigm situation where MBIA adopting 'marking-to-market' accounting resulted in

---

[90] This idea was based on Holgate, P, Accounting for Lawyers (Cambridge: Cambridge University Press, 2006) p.117, 118.
[91] Langendijk, H, Swagerman, D, Verhoog, W, Is Fair Value Fair? (Chichester: John Wiley & Son Ltd, The Atrium, 2003) pp 256.
[92] Id.
[93] Id.
[94] Plender, J. (2008) "Financial crisis presents a test for fair value accounting", Financial Times, available at http://www.ft.com/home/uk, accessed 4th March 2008.

rigorous weaknesses of its balance sheets. But a strongly held view at one European central bank is that it is not "mark-to-market" accounting that is to blame for severe weaknesses in banks' balance sheets but that prices of MBS securities have fallen to levels that imply unrealistically high rates of default. And therein lies the problem, which lies not with marking-to-market as such but with its use to underpin pro-cyclical bank capital requirements – for it is the capital regime that should be reviewed.

In theory, mark-to-market accounting serves not only as a means of keeping investors informed, it also underlies the balance sheet and hence generates that principle figure which regulates a bank's activity: "its capital ratio".[95] The standard Basel II[96] requirement is that a bank's target capital ratio, as measured against risk-weighted assets, should be 8 per cent.[97] The

---

[95] Basel II: International Convergence of Capital Measurement and Capital Standards: A Revised Framework available at http://www.bis.org.
[96] Id.
[97] Basel II establishes minimum capital requirements for financial institutions in the areas of credit, market, and operational risk. The minimum total regulatory capital (own funds) is 8%, which can be calculated as follows: For example

Institute of International Finance pointed out "the dangers of mark-to-market accounting at times of illiquidity in creating a vicious circle of forced asset sales, lower prices, further writedowns and more asset sales",[98] an argument which supports the answer to the main question of this project. The implementation of mark-to-market may create instant losses, which force banks to either cut back on lending or raise more funds, and hence trigger a spiral downturn in prices.

Another problem arises when trading financial instruments in illiquid markets. "Barth and Landsman (1995) make the observation that in absence of active, liquid markets, fair value is not well defined in the sense that an instrument's acquisition, price, selling price, and value-in-use to the entity can differ from each other".[99] A good example of the struggle of

the bank exposure under 1 year has a risk weight of 15%
For an exposure of £500,000 – the risk-weighted assets are equal to 15% or £75,000
The minimum capital requirement under Basel II is 8% of £75,000 or £6,000.
[98] Guha, K, (2008) "Banks take blame for credit crisis", Financial Times, available at http://www.ft.com/home/uk, accessed 9th April 2008.
[99] Barth and Landsman (1995) as cited in Bhat, G. (2008) "Risk Relevance of Fair Value Gains and Losses, and the Impact of

financial institutions in valuing illiquid instruments is "AIG, the US insurance giant, which announced in February 2008 almost $5bn of writedowns after it adjusted some of the assumptions it used to value certain securities linked to subprime loans".[100]

A criticism that has been made against changing direction from "historic cost"[101] is that it will uncover losses on loans, which can have a negative impact on the banking sector affected by a credit crunch. This has not stopped the European Commission mandating through the Capital Requirements Directive that institutions must ensure that "the value applied to each of its trading book positions appropriately reflects the current market value".[102] The directive emphasises that market value is a measurement based on market data

---

Disclosure and Corporate Governance", Rotman School of Management, University of Toronto, available at http://ssrn.com accessed 7th March 2008.

[100] Hughes, J. "Concept of 'fair value' ignores stench of the real world", Financial Times, 2008, available at http://www.ft.com/home/uk, accessed 4th April 2008.

[101] For a fuller discussion see Davies, P. (2008) "Insight: True impact of mark-to-market on the credit crisis", Financial Times, available at http://www.ft.com/home/uk, accessed 28th March 2008.

[102] See Directive 2006/49/EC, Chapter IV, Section 5, Article 33.

from an independent valuation; the question is whether investors will trust an independent "market price"[103] or rather a "management's potentially subjective view of the value".[104]

The CRD establishes that the rules related to verification of profits must be in accordance with the principles set out in Directive 86/635/EEC, which introduced "two standard profit-and-loss account layouts and special provisions on certain items in the profit-and-loss account such as interest receivable, income from securities, net profit or loss on financial operations, etc.".[105] One could argue that under these rules fair value measures based on market value of asset and liabilities can be subjective, as more market values will be estimated. The use of these figures undoubtedly will influence the earnings and trading books of financial institutions, therefore there is a danger that creditworthiness of financial reports may

---

[103] Hughes, J, Concept of 'fair value' ignores stench of the real world, Financial Times, 2008, available at
http://www.ft.com/home/uk, accessed 4th April 2008.
[104] Id.
[105] Directive 86/635/EC of 8 December 1986 on the annual accounts and consolidated accounts of banks and other financial institutions.

decline, along with their profit margins.

According to this new framework profits based on fair value are not "unrealised profits",[106] leaving room for doubt to investors and shareholders.[107] Professor Hoogendoorn (2003) affirmed that "in the case of a valuation of all assets and liabilities at fair value, the shareholders' value does not reflect the value of the company".[108] This situation is reflected in the fact that the company is affected by different factors[109] that are not reflected in the balance sheet, and it can be said that those factors may influence the risk situation of the company and it could be a disadvantage for investors and shareholders.

Another issue related to profits based on fair value is the possibility of tax unfairness as "the starting point for tax assessment is the profit shown in the company's annual statutory accounts".[110] From 2005

---

[106] The Institute of Chartered Accountants, Fair Value Accounting available at www.icaew.co.uk.

[107] Id.

[108] Langendijk, H, Swagerman, D, Verhoog, W, Is Fair Value Fair? (Chichester: John Wiley & Son Ltd, The Atrium, 2003) pp 125.

[109] E.g. capital, good will, etc.

[110] Holgate, P, Accounting for Lawyers (Cambridge: Cambridge

UK institutions had to start using the IFRS rules for consolidated accounts, which are the rules followed by the European Commission. While it would undoubtedly be in the interest of some financial institutions to show an increase in their profit margins, for others payment of corporation tax may increase as a consequence, and may affect the revenue of those financial institutions.

Valuation of Debt

According to Professor Hoogendoorn "the weakest point in the application of fair value is the valuation of debt particularly when credit rates are changing".[111] Imagine that a credit institution has taken out a medium- or long-term loan paying to the bank 6.5%, but due to deterioration of financial circumstances the institution has to borrow money one year later paying market rates, say 8.5%; there is an advantage

University Press, 2006) p.114

[111] Langendijk, H, Swagerman, D, Verhoog, W, Is Fair Value Fair? (Chichester: John Wiley & Son Ltd, The Atrium, 2003) pp 125.

regarding the first loan already agreed at 6.5%; but the question remains as to whether the changing circumstances (e.g. deterioration of the company) which may affect the goodwill, are going to be reflected in the fair value calculations.[112]

The present financial turmoil presents good examples of corporate loan rates rising in line with "inter-bank rates".[113] The crisis can be encapsulated by two scenarios which, taken together, will change forever the lending structure in the financial market. In the first place, credit institutions which find themselves unable to sell their asset-backed securities may be forced to adjust their lending mechanisms instead. Secondly, opportunities may arise for those financial institutions for which "potential funding liabilities to vehicles or conduits are small as a proportion of their balance sheet".[114] While some credit institutions are not willing to lend money, others are waiting for the right moment to take

---

[112]Ibid. Based on Professor Hoogendoorn's example.
[113] Bank of England. (2007) "Turmoil in Financial Markets: What Can Central Banks Do?, available at www.lexisnexis.com.uk accessed 22th December 2007.
[114] Id.

advantage of the opportunities arising from the flotation of assets at heavily discounted prices, even though some financial instruments may be withdrawn from the market altogether.

Is fair value too far from cash?

Given that "assets in business generate cash flows jointly, not separately",[115] another issue to be considered is whether the fair value of individual assets will reflect the future cash flow of financial institutions. Findings from the study of Keji Chen, Gregory A. Sommers and Gary K. Taylor (2006) concluded that "achieving fair value accounting would reduce the ability of financial accounting to predict future cash flows". [116] Fair value, then, can be seen as a practical problem in accounting. It seems that the

---

[115] The Institute of Chartered Accountants. (2007) "Fair Value Accounting", available at www.icaew.co.uk.

[116] Chen, K, Sommers, G, Taylor, G. (2006) "Fair Value's Affect on Accounting's Ability to Predict Future Cash Flows: A Glance Back and a Look at the Potential Impact of Reaching the Goal", available at SSRN: http://ssrn.com/abstract=930702, accessed 10 October 2007.

estimates of fair value are far from cash, and that can affect the accountability of credit institutions under the current financial crisis, influenced by the fact that some banks have taken on too much debt.[117]

A recent study carried out by Gauri Bhat of the University of Toronto (2008) discusses the deficiency of evidence attributed to reliability concerns related to fair values.[118] Two main sources feed the 'reliability concerns', according to this study. Firstly, financial instruments are risky, and this presents the possibility that some values that differ from estimated fair values can be released.[119] Secondly, estimation of fair values is more often than not highly subjective.[120] These concerns are based on how reliable is the calculation

---

[117] ...debt is a highly complex contract. This is because debt entails a promise to repay principal and interest on a loan or advance – a promise whose fulfilment is by its nature uncertain and will differ among borrowers.: Davies, EP, Debt, Fragility and Systemic Risk (United States: Oxford University Press, 1992) pp 4.

[118] Bhat, G. (2008) "Risk Relevance of Fair Value Gains and Losses, and the Impact of Disclosure and Corporate Governance", Rotman School of Management, University of Toronto, available at SSRN: http://ssrn.com, accessed 7th March 2008.

[119] Id.

[120] Id.

of fair value based on market variables within financial instruments – a process which in future may involve much in the way of trial and error.

It's worthwhile to briefly expand on this here. In academic literature, a conclusion that is based on misinterpretation or drawn out of context or without due regard to all the pertinent facts is rightly regarded as an error – a bald mistake. In empirical science however, 'error'[121] is regarded as unavoidable, an inevitable by-product of empirical measurement. Measurements always contain errors and therefore uncertainties, hence scientific empiricism has been forced to develop and integrate sophisticated methodologies and statistical techniques for coping with error. Indeed, it seems unlikely that science would have achieved such lofty heights without such compensatory mechanisms in place.

Validity is particularly important in considering the reliability of estimated fair values. The Accounting

---

[121] In science the word "error" does not carry the usual connotations of "mistake" or "blunder". "Error" in a scientific measurement means the inevitable uncertainty that attends all measurements: Semyon, R, Measurement error and uncertainties: theory and practice (New York: AIP Press, c2000) at pp 3.

Standards Board (ASB), in its response to the IASB's 'Fair Value Measurements' expressed "considerable doubts over the validity of basing the fair value of a liability on a market transfer".[122] Under the present credit crisis conditions, lack of reliable information that realistically expresses the risk of credit institutions can be one source of where the problem of fair value lies.

According to the CRD the "degree of risk" [123] assumed by credit institutions has to be reflected in the minimum capital requirements laid down with assets-value and off-balance-sheet instruments. It is important to mention at this point that the degree of risk has been fed by the lending growth of the financial market, which has been based on rising asset prices.[124] This development in the market gives rise to difficulties when it comes to applying the new

---

[122] ASB responds to IAS on Discussion Paper – 'Fair Value Measurements', Accounting Standard Board, 2007, available at http://lexisnexis.com/uk accessed 10th October 2007.

[123] See Directive 2006/49/EC.

[124] To expand this idea see Davies, P. (2008) "Insight: True impact of market-to-market on the credit crisis", Financial Times, available at http://www.ft.com/home/uk, accessed 4th April 2008.

regulations under the new Directive, because the uncovering of losses may naturally reflect problems faced at present by financial institutions – and is therefore likely to scare off potential buyers.

It could be argued that under CRD regulations the disclosure of fair values reflecting the risk assumed by credit institutions can have, and indeed are having, a destructive impact under the current market conditions. Some commentators argue that "fair value accounting"[125] will generate a phenomenon by expanding the balance sheets, which was caused in the first place by "the most blatant excesses of US mortgage lending".[126] It seems that the rules need to be re-written; regulations need to address the accountability of owners of financial institutions, as they have in their hands the real possibility of changing the lending structures.

---

[125] Id.

[126] The collapse of the subprime market is attributable to many factors…, the related embrace by the Securities and Exchange Commission (SEC) and the Financial Accounting Standards Board (FASB) of "fair value accounting," an ill-advised change in reporting standards…: Whalen, C. (2008) "The Subprime Crisis - Cause, Effect and Consequences," at http://papers.ssrn.com accessed 5th April 2008.

But paradoxically, while some are waiting for fresh opportunities that will inevitably result from this crisis the only accountable party for potential loss appears to be the tax-payer.

TOXIC ASSETS [127]

---

[127] Ingram Pinn illustration available at http://search.ft.com, accessed 17th October 2008

CAPITAL REQUIREMENTS DIRECTIVE AND PRUDENTIAL SUPERVISION

The Capital Requirements Directive will place EU countries under the microscope of prudential supervision, which can be exercised at a solo entity level (as one separated company) or at a consolidated level (as a group of companies). As some of the European financial institutions are already committed to consolidated supervision, this new regulation may not disturb the financial sector; however, difficulties may arise in situations where the parent company is not based in the EU, as financial practices can differ from one country to another.

For an effective supervision between Member States 'mutual cooperation' is vital.[128] According to the Directive MSs have the duty to provide the information to facilitate the monitoring of financial institutions, in particular with regard to liquidity, solvency, deposit guarantees, the limiting of large exposures, administrative and accounting procedures, and internal control mechanisms.[129] The drive to establish cooperation across the European countries, and that this will permit supervision to proceed smoothly, would appear to be based on the assumption that the new regulations will be interpreted and applied evenly across the region. Yet such an outcome seems unlikely given the difficulties that are bound to arise as a result of incorporating the regulations into pre-existing – and often diverse – regimes.

For example, in 2006 plans were made in Poland for a unified financial services supervisory agency, which opened the possibility for political intervention. Christoph Rosenberg, senior regional representative

---

[128] Directive 2006/48/EC, Title V, Chapter I, Section1, art. 41.
[129] Ibid. Title V, Chapter I, Section1, art. 42.

for the IMF, affirmed that "one fundamental objective of any law setting up such an agency is to ensure that its activity is independent of any government's political agenda. Without such assurances, undue interference could weaken banks, hurt investor confidence in the zloty and even result in financial crises".[130] It seems clear that the degree of discretion in the interpretation of the new EC regulation can vary from country to country and that this lack of harmonisation could weaken the implementation process, with inevitable repercussions for supervision across Member States.

---

[130] Cienski, J. (2006) "Unified financial services supervisory agency", Financial Times, available at http://search.ft.com accessed 24 March 2008.

Supervisory Approach

Prudential supervision seeks to introduce a "supervisory approach",[131] in which bank examiners focus less on compliance with specific regulatory rules and the risks of the financial instruments currently in the bank's portfolios, and more on the soundness of a credit institution.[132] Regulation is basically relying on estimation of a credit institution's risk, as a warning mechanism to prevent a financial failure. In the present financial turmoil, allowing banks to estimate their own credit risk would appear not to be an effective measure against risk from large exposures.

Charlie McCreevy, the internal markets commissioner, urged the various European institutions - the Commission, Council, and parliament - to reach agreement on changes to the so-called Basel II capital requirements directive by April 2009.[133]

---

[131] To expand this concept see Mishkin, F, Prudential Supervision: Why is it important and what are the issues? (Cambridge, US: National Bureau of Research, Inc., 2000) pp 16.
[132] Id.
[133] Larsen, P, Tait, N. (2008) "EU warning systems 'need

Undoubtedly this is an issue that needs to be addressed by the European Financial institutions and EC Commission, as the supervisory approach introduced by the CRD is not the remedy needed for the illness of the financial sector; a more radical structural change in the regulations may have to be introduced to achieve market recovery.

Continuing with the discussion on the supervisory approach of the CRD, the fact is that home Member States are responsible to oversee the solvency of their financial institutions while the supervision of the liquidity of the branches and monetary policies is the responsibility of the host Member State's competent authorities. On the one hand, this dual approach can have a positive effect on the supervision of market risk, especially if it oversees a larger number of EU institutions, including institutions that used to be exempt from supervision. On the other hand, difficulties could arise out of bureaucracy and a lack of clarity in which this approach is implemented across Member States.

strengthening"', Financial Times, available at http://search.ft.com accessed 6th April 2008.

Another aspect highlighted by prudential supervision is the 'protection of clients'.[134] According to Mishkin, if more public information is available about the risks incurred by banks and the quality of their portfolio, market discipline can be enhanced by enabling creditors and investors to assess and monitor banks and so act as a deterrent to excessive risk taking.[135] This is a difficult task when banks don't trust each other, or indeed their clients; the philosophy behind CRD legislation seems divorced from reality, as the priority for the regulators is to protect the interest of financial institutions, particularly from the consequences of the "credit squeeze".[136]

The Directive relies on prudential supervision to minimise the failure of credit institutions that can affect the stability of the market. Minsky defined

---

[134] The processing of clients' data should be in accordance with the rules on transfer of personal data according to the Council Directive 95/46/EC on the protection of individuals with regard to the processing of personal data and the free movement of such data.

[135] To expand this concept see Mishkin, F, Prudential Supervision: Why is it important and what are the issues? (Cambridge, US: National Bureau of Research, Inc., 2000) pp 14.

[136] Larsen, P, Tait, N. (2008) "EU warning systems 'need strengthening'", Financial Times, available at http://search.ft.com accessed 6th April 2008.

systemic fragility as "an indispensable attribute of the financial system, which results from the normal function of the economy".[137] Under the present "pressures in global markets",[138] where credit institutions are "interconnected",[139] the failure of a large bank like Bear Sterns could have triggered a domino effect under the current financial fragility;[140] therefore emergency provisions of funding were necessary from the Federal Bank, this reflects that

...at least at a moment of extreme market fragility - some institutions are too interconnected to fail. This includes the main investment banks that are active participants in bilateral credit derivative markets and the triparty repo market.[141]

---

[137] Nesvetailova, A, Fragile Finance, (Basingstoke: Pelgrave Macmillan, 2007) pp 59.

[138] To expand this concept see Bollen, B. (2008) "Less risk, more kudos on the stock exchange", Financial Times, available at http://search.ft.com accessed 7th April 2008.

[139] Guha, K. (2008) "Experts speculate on unorthodox policy measures", Financial Times, available at http://search.ft.com accessed 7th April 2008.

[140] To expand see Financial Fragility: case study: Davies, EP, Debt, Fragility and Systemic Risk (United States: Oxford University Press, 1992) pp 110-111.

[141] Guha, K. (2008) "Experts speculate on unorthodox policy measures", Financial Times, available at http://search.ft.com

The failure of Bear Sterns demonstrates that pumping liquidity into the institution has proved to be a more effective measure than supervision. The reliance on prudential supervision to minimise instability in the market is a big problem if the supervision fails to assess effectively the risks and solvency of institutions, as could have been the case in the failure of Northern Rock.

The credit crunch has prompted a massive intervention from central banks, which have injected liquidity into the financial sector.

It stems from an 'overhang' on banks' balance sheets of assets in which markets have closed . . . That has created uncertainty about the strength of banks' financial positions.[142]

Under the current financial fragility, the financial sector in Europe and the US welcomes the support from central banks to raise funding rates for credit institutions. In the Eurozone tension is rising as banks are due to report for the end of the first

---

accessed 7th April 2008.
[142]Financial Times. (2008) "Not yet time for a bail-out of banks", available at http://search.ft.com accessed 28 March 2008.

quarter. The European Central Bank "said it was closely monitoring liquidity conditions" and "stands ready to provide additional liquidity if needed".[143] It seems that regulations and regulators are treading two different paths – while regulations are based on credit risk assessment, regulators are dealing with liquidity and solvency issues. Indeed, it is difficult to escape the conclusion that the financial sector is still in need of more effective regulation, lack of which largely explains how the financial sector found itself rocked by the credit crisis in the first place.

Supervisors

The Committee of European Banking Supervisors has the duty to assist the Commission in the implementation of the CRD and the supervision of financial institutions throughout the Community[144]. The Committee must work within the framework of

---

[143] Mackenzie, M, Atkins, R. (2008) "Central banks act to calm financial markets", Financial Times available at http://search.ft.com accessed 28 March 2008.
[144] See Directive 2006/48/EC, para. (55).

the Directive and apply the regulations to all relevant institutions. Competent authorities must exercise the supervisory functions but under the uncertainty of the present financial crisis in the past few weeks, "politicians and regulators - including Alistair Darling, the UK chancellor - have recommended the use of so-called 'colleges' of regulators to supervise large multinational banking groups".[145] Not very surprisingly, a framework that has just been implemented now needs to be amended, as it seems that the legislative structure in place is not strong enough to resist the destructive spiral power of this financial tornado.

Supervisors will have a duty to assess the performance of financial institutions and the disclosure of such information on one hand can be valuable to improve investments and shareholders' returns and therefore to promote public confidence; but on the other hand, supervision can be subjective and far from accurate in reflecting the true risk

---

[145] Larsen, P, Tait, N. (2008) "EU warning systems 'need strengthening'", Financial Times, available at http://search.ft.com accessed 6th April 2008.

exposure of financial institutions. In light of the current credit crisis[146] the public exposure of accounts reports of some banks could be counterproductive as it may affect economic growth, and this could prove problematic for supervisory agents.

Another obstacle that supervisors may encounter is "too little power to act effectively".[147] Supervisors are expected to have enough knowledge of the institutions, the role they play in the market, and have sufficient powers to apply adequate supervisory techniques and reporting in order for the institution to introduce correcting measures at the right time. Inevitably though, effective supervision will find itself operating in the face of tremendous pressure as financial institutions are, by definition, acting under various stressors such as competition[148], profit

---

[146] ...market people and officialdom said that we are not in a "crisis", but a very long process of deleveraging and distress: Dizard, J. (2008) "Raising equity is top of to-do list", Financial Times available at http://search.ft.com accessed 24 March 2008.

[147] Ward, J. (2002) "The Supervisory Approach: A critique", ESRC Centre for Business Research, pp 4.

[148] One effect of competition is for firms to seek to distinguish themselves from others: Goodhart, CAE, The Emerging Framework of Financial Regulation (London: Central Banking Publication Ltd., 1998).

maximisation, market share value, etc., that can influence the way financial institutions allow supervisors to carry out their duties. These conditions almost certainly will complicate the supervision process even further and may, in some cases, directly result in supervisory failures.

Supervision in Crisis

Since the introduction of the Financial Services Act 1986 the UK financial market has witnessed the collapse of Britain's Barings Bank,[149] the personal pensions' mis-selling scandal,[150] the endowment mortgage scandal[151], and recently the Northern Rock

[149] Barings plc (In liquidation) & Anor v Coopers & Lybrand (A firm) & Ors: Barings Futures (Singapore) Pte Ltd (In liquidation) v Mattar & 36 Ors (2003).
[150] See Re Maxwell Communications Corporation plc, Homan v Vogel [1994] BCC 741. An application was made to inspect documents relating to the failure of the Maxwell companies. See also MGN Pension Trustees Ltd v Bank of America National Trust and Savings Association and another (Serious Fraud Office intervening); Bishopsgate Investment Management Ltd v Crédit Suisse (Serious Fraud Office intervening) [1995] 2 All ER 355.
[151] Id.

crisis[152]; these events among others suggest that the regulatory system is not exercising effective control over a financial sector driven by increased rate of profit margins and the rapid trading made possible with new technology. The case of Barings provides a stark illustration that a bank can be driven into insolvency within a very short timescale, even with supervisory structures in place.

Under the present UK legislative structure the Financial Services Authorities, FSA,[153] shares the responsibility for overseeing the functioning of the markets with the Bank of England and the Treasury.[154] "When the collapse of Northern Rock occurred no one was in charge, Mervyn King, Bank governor, was forced into a rapid u-turn on intervention; Alistair Darling, the chancellor, was panicked into guaranteeing all the Rock's deposits, committing the taxpayer to

---

[152] Betts, P. (2007) "A history lesson in the wake of Northern Rock crisis", Financial Times available at http://search.ft.com accessed 24 March 2008.

[153] Previous Self- Regulatory Organisations: SIB, IMRO, LAUTRO, FIMBRA, PIA.

[154] Amery, P. (2008) "Too heavy financial regulation has created danger", Financial Times, available at http://search.ft.com accessed 24 March 2008.

enormous liabilities; and the FSA was found asleep on the job as bank supervisor".[155] The failure of Northern Rock proved that supervision based on regulatory rules is not efficient; and furthermore that the paternalistic attitude of the UK government may lead to moral hazard situations, as other financial institutions may act irresponsibly assuming that state protection will be available 'on the tax payer'. The FSA will be in charge of implementing the new CRD, the question remains as to whether the enforcement of these new regulations would, or could, prevent a crisis in the future similar to that which engulfed Northern Rock.[156]

Another issue that can affect the supervision system is the collapse of markets in collateralized debt obligations and collateralized loan obligations, which were created to allow banks to shift the risk off-balance sheet and avoid capital charges, while satisfying the appetite of hungry investors affected by

---

[155] Id.
[156] Yorulmazer, T. (2008) "Liquidity, Bank Runs and Bailouts: Spillover Effects During the Northern Rock Episode1", Federal Reserve Bank of New York available at http://papers.ssrn.com accessed 25 March 2008.

a decrease in profit rates.[157] In this developmental trend within the market some credit institutions may find themselves in a double-bind, operating under immense pressure on the one hand to raise money and increase profit rates, while on the other trying to cope with legislation which presses them "to hold internal capital adequate in 'quantity, quality and distribution'".[158]

---

[157] This idea was based on Sullivan, R. (2007) "Regional Profit Rates of National Banks and the Development of the U.S. Financial Market, 1870-1914", Federal Reserve Bank of Kansas City, available at SSRN: http://papers.ssrn.com accessed 25 March 2008.

[158] See Directive 2006/48/EC, para. (29).

Impact of Minimum Capital Requirements

The minimum capital requirements[159] as set up by the CRD play a central role in the supervision of credit institutions and in the assessment of their main risks, such as credit risks, market risks, operational and liquidity risks. It would appear that the framework would be desperately welcome under the current financial turmoil but, perhaps unsurprisingly, calls have already been made for the framework to be adjusted.[160]

However, the directive tries to improve market confidence via prudential supervision, the main principle is that "adequate solvency"[161] should weigh up assets and off-balance-sheet items according to the degree of risk taken by the institution.[162] "Off-balance sheet accounting practices has been blamed for

---

[159] The Directive 2006/48/EC set up minimum capital requirements.

[160] "In an interim report endorsed by Group of Seven finance ministers meeting in Tokyo, the Financial Stability Forum warned that the full impact of the credit squeeze had yet to be felt." Soble, J. (2008) "Full impact of squeeze 'has yet to be felt'", Financial Times at http://search.ft.com accessed 22 March 2008.

[161] Directive 2006/48/EC, para. (36).

[162] Id.

potentially obscuring the true risks that banks face".[163] As this paper is written, Ambac, a bond insurer, revealed its recapitalisation plan for $1.5bn (£755m),[164] which meant a loss of nearly a fifth of its stock market value, disappointing investors and shareholders.

Ambac has been racing to find capital because its triple-A credit ratings have been threatened by losses on guarantees it made on securities backed by subprime mortgages and other assets.[165]

The prudential supervision measures can be conflicting as the directive wants to lay down common minimum capital requirements across the European Community at times when some of the world's biggest banks are facing massive losses, solvency[166] problems, and are in need of recapitalisation.

---

[163] Hughes, J. (2008) "Companies face being forced to reveal off-balance sheet vehicles", Financial Times at http://search.ft.com accessed 22 March 2008.

[164] Van Duyn, A, Guerrera, F, White, B, in, Ambac shares lose almost a fifth over $1.5bn recapitalisation plan, 2008, Financial Times at http://search.ft.com accessed 22 March 2008.

[165] Van Duyn, A, Guerrera, F, White, B, in, Ambac shares lose almost a fifth over $1.5bn recapitalisation plan, 2008, Financial Times at http://search.ft.com accessed 22 March 2008.

[166] Several building societies had to be merged with larger institutions when loan losses resulting from earlier imprudent lending cast their liquidity or solvency into question: Davies, EP, Debt, Fragility and Systemic Risk (United States: Oxford University Press, 1992) pp 113.

Transparency vs. Discretion

In light of the CRD, transparency[167] is an attempt to restore confidence and effectiveness in the operation of the financial market.[168] The Directive not only refers to the transparency of credit institutions but also to that of competent supervisory authorities. One possible reason why efforts to restore market confidence have failed so far is the ongoing "uncertainty"[169] about the solvency of financial institutions.[170] As a result of the uncertain changes in the present economic environment, the Financial Services Authority is currently facing criticisms for its

---

[167] See also Directive 2004/109/EC of 15 of December on the harmonisation of transparency requirements in relation to information about issuers whose securities are admitted to trading on a regulated market and amending Directive 2001/34/EC.

[168] See Directive 2006/48/EC para. (61).

[169] There is no precise economic theory as to how decisions are made under uncertainty: Davies, EP, Debt, Fragility and Systemic Risk (United States: Oxford University Press, 1992) pp 135.

[170] This idea is based on Mayers, J. (2008) "Markets just could not self-correct", Financial Times, available at http://search.ft.com accessed 7th April 2008.

failure in properly handling the supervision of Northern Rock, the UK mortgage lender that was nationalised at the beginning of 2008.

The watchdog is expected to admit that its focus on customer protection and other "conduct of business" issues may have come at the expense of some prudential duties overseeing the viability of banks' business models.[171]

The difficulties faced by the FSA in the case of Northern Rock provide a stark reminder that transparency is not only difficult to achieve because of the complexity of the new financial regulations but also due to "the discretion exercised by the management of institutions they supervise".[172]

Under the new regulatory framework credit institutions can exercise discretion using their own risk models for setting capital requirements.[173] Sheila

---

[171] Hughes, J., Goff, S. (2008) "FSA to admit mistakes in handling Rock", Financial Times available at http://search.ft.com accessed 25 March 2008.

[172] Id.

[173] For fuller discussion see Mishkin, F, Prudential Supervision: Why is it important and what are the issues? (Cambridge, US: National Bureau of Research, Inc., 2000) pp 17.

Bair, chairman of the Federal Deposit Insurance Corporation in the US, recently noted that "these models had important weaknesses which, in the light of today's market turmoil, were a flashing yellow light to drive carefully".[174] A fundamental problem is that CRD regulations create incentives that can undermine credit risk because credit institutions are allowed to use their own internal models to assess the risk and they have the discretion to establish the amount of regulatory capital, which can leave room for excessive risk taking.

---

[174] Harald Benink, H. and Kaufman, G. (2008) "Turmoil reveals the inadequacy of Basel II", Financial Times available at http://search.ft.com accessed 25 March 2008.

The Meaning of 'Spiral Death'

Definition by Prof. Dr. Joseph Tanega[175]

Positive feedback works like this: A gives some X to B, and B gives even more X to A, and so with each iteration, you get more and more X until something explodes! The 'spiral death' idea works the same way, except you get less and less. In the credit crisis, subprime MBS started off with AAA rating. But then people started to find out that the obligors were not as good as they were purported to be, so the value of the instruments went down to the point that nobody wants to buy them. Then these AAA MBS are stuck on the bank's books. The question is, how do you value them? The accounting rules say they have to be valued according to 'fair value' – that is, according to any

---

[175] The Meaning of "Spiral Death" was written by Dr Joseph Tanega on 11th April 2008 as a contribution for the Dissertation "A Critique of the EU Capital Requirements Directive in Light of the Lessons Learned or not Learned in the 2007-2008 Credit Crisis" by Beatriz McCarron (University of Westminster 2008)

observable price. Since there is no observable price, they should be marked down. So, even though the AAA MBS have not been sold in the market, they are marked down. Since the banks are required to hold a certain amount of capital against risky assets (according to CRD) with the failure of the AAA MBS, suddenly they will need to raise capital because the value of their capital has suddenly gone down. So then they are forced to sell some of their best capital into the market in a kind of fire sale, which brings the price of all like-for-like collateral down. This is the meaning of spiral death. It is essentially a matter of forced sales of the best collateral, which in turns reduces the value of the bank's collateral, which in turn forces the bank to sell even more collateral, et hoc genus omne.

Downward Spiral

Debt underpins the 'credit crunch' dynamic that befell Bear Stearns in 2008 (and Northern Rock a year earlier). Fears that it was exposed to the crisis in US mortgage debt meant that nobody was willing to lend Bear Stearns money. It rapidly found that it could not raise the necessary funds to service its debts and tumbled to the ground. Even an emergency lending facility was not sufficient to save the bank and it was eventually sold off to JP Morgan for a mere $236 million.[176] Before the advent of the credit crisis, it had been valued at over $140 billion.[177] In a desperate bid to stop the crisis spreading, the Federal Reserve – which also doubles as the main financial regulator in the US – made an emergency cut[178] in the interest it

---

[176] Goldstein, M. (2008) "JPMorgan Buys Bear on the Cheap", Business Week, available at http://www.businessweek.com, accessed 6[tH] April 2008.

[177] Goldstein, M. (2008) "JPMorgan Buys Bear on the Cheap", Business Week, available at http://www.businessweek.com, accessed 6[tH] April 2008.

[178] The Federal Reserve on Sunday (7th of April 2008) cut the discount rate for banks by 25 basis points to 3.25 per cent and

charged to other banks. It also announced plans for a new credit facility for investment banks. The last time the Federal Reserve acted likewise was during the Great Depression of the 1930s.[179]

The Fed said bank borrowing from the discount window averaged $7bn in the week to April 2 – a $6.5bn jump from the previous week. The total amount outstanding on April 2 was $10.3bn.[180]

Meanwhile, borrowing from the new emergency finance facility for primary dealers – including investment banks that do not have access to the discount window – rose $5.2bn to average $38.1bn over the week, though the amount outstanding dipped to $34.4bn on April 2.[181]

---

created a new lending facility for other financial institutions in an attempt to boost market liquidity: Sevastopulo, D. (2008) "Fed cuts bank rate to boost confidence", Financial Times, available at http://search.ft.com, accessed 10th April 2008.

[179] Eichengreen, B, Mitchener, K. (2003) "The Great Depression as a credit boom gone wrong", Bank of International Settlements, available at SSRN: http://papers.ssrn.com, accessed 9th April 2008.

[180] Guha, K. (2008) US ban borrowing from Fed, Financial Times, available at http://search.ft.com, accessed 7th April 2008.

[181] Id.

The problem that brought about the collapse of Bear Stearns and Northern Rock is not unique to those institutions. Most banks are highly leveraged, they lend out far more than the amount of capital invested in them. Now this debt bubble has burst, with disastrous consequences for the system as a whole. The crisis has already engulfed Northern Rock and Bear Stearns as well as a variety of less well-known names such as hedge funds Peloton Capital[182] and the Carlyle Capital Corporation.[183] Each casualty makes the lenders even more cautious, forcing leveraged investors to present more capital up front – and this in turn invokes such groups to sell off their investments, thus propelling a downward spiral in values of financial instruments.

---

[182] Talk about a high-risk hedge fund and most people assume it is a tautology. This year's sudden collapses of the $2bn flagship fund of London's Peloton Partners and the $1bn New York-based Focus Capital, as well as a raft of smaller funds, has done nothing to change that view: Mackintosh, M. (2008) "Back to the roots with a high-risk hedge fund", Financial Times, available at http://search.ft.com, accessed 10th April 2008.

[183] Arnold, M. (2008) "Fed just made matters worse, says Carlyle", Financial Times, available at http://search.ft.com, accessed 10th April 2008.

...the US Federal Reserve was supposed to ease the liquidity crisis for struggling financial groups such as Carlyle Capital Corporation. But David Rubenstein, co-founder of the Carlyle Group, said it only accelerated the demise of his group's mortgage-backed securities fund, which is being liquidated by its banks for defaulting on more than $16bn of debts only eight months after listing on Euronext Amsterdam.[184]

Another relevant example for this study is the case between insurers Sphere Drake and brokers Sterling Cook Browne,[185] which

...had considerable implications for others drawn into the transactions collectively called the "Unicover Spiral", a series of heavily loss making reinsurances of American Personal accident insurances such as workman's compensation.[186]

---

[184] Id.

[185] In the case of Sphere Drake Insurance Ltd and another v Euro International Underwriting Ltd and others [2003] EWHC 1636 the court ruled that: The market which traded in losses with which the action was concerned was one in which no rational and honest person would have participated if he had understood the market and proper disclosure had been made. The market was obviously unsustainable.

[186] Sphere Drake court decision favours underwriters available at http://www.maritimelondon.com/london_matters/18uly03_main.shtml, accessed 28th February 2008.

Death spiral convertibles differ from normal convertibles in that they are "bonds that can be converted into a fixed number of shares at an agreed conversion price".[187] As the share price spirals down the conversion ratio changes accordingly, "the lower the share price, the higher the number of shares that the company must issue".[188] The rationale behind the death spiral of convertibles is to protect the bondholder in the event that share prices do not increase. In the actual financial crisis "about one in five junk bond issues is currently trading at distressed levels", [189] this suggests that the financial sector is doomed to invoke 'death spirals' out of desperation to raise money amid market pressure.

---

[187] Mitchell, L. (2006) "Convertible Bond that offers lifeline to some small companies", Financial Times, available at http://search.ft.com, accessed 24th March 2008.

[188] Id.

[189] For fuller discussion see Chancellor, E. (2008) "A new-found respect for uncertainty", Financial Times, available at http://search.ft.com, accessed 9th April 2008.

CONCLUSION

*How on earth did this potentially very serious
crisis come about?*

Capitalism is based on profit. Capitalist enterprises
which make a profit are able to invest and compete
effectively, while those which fail to make a profit go
to the wall – this is the ultimate law of competition.
But it is not simply the amount of profit that matters;
the crucial yardstick is the rate of profit[190] – how
many pence (or cents, kopecs, etc.) are returned for

---

[190] See Sullivan, R. (2007) "Regional Profit Rates of National
Banks and the Development of the U.S. Financial Market, 1870-
1914", Federal Reserve Bank of Kansas City, available at SSRN:
http://papers.ssrn.com, accessed 8th April 2008.

each pound (or dollar, rouble, etc.) invested. "Profit rates are germane to the mechanism of capital allocation because they are critical incentives for entry to and exit from the financial market".[191] A fall in this rate of profit calls into question the viability of the entire system.

In the 1950s and 1960s[192] capitalism enjoyed a sustained boom based on high profit rates. But in the 1970s and 1980s the profit rate fell by approximately half in most major economies.[193] In recent years some of this fall has been recovered in some countries, most notably the US, due largely to a massive increase in productivity across the industrial sector. However, the underlying system has not been fundamentally

---

[191] Id.

[192] Barry Eichengreen, professor of economics at the University of California, Berkeley, argued recently in The European Economy Since 1945 that, while western Europe had enjoyed a "golden age" in the 1950s and 1960s, the political and social institutions of the post second world war era were better suited to incremental change rather than radical innovation. As cited in Atkins, R. (2008) "Heightened resistance? Eurozone 'decoupling' from US economy will be put to the test", Financial Times, available at http://search.ft.com, accessed 9th April 2008.

[193] Dumenil, G, Lévy, D. (2001) "The Profit Rate: Where and How Much Did it Fall? Did It Recover? (USA 1948-1997)", Review of Radical Political Economics, available at http://www.ingentaconnect.com, accessed 6th April 2008.

restructured, and profit rates have not recovered to levels seen in the 1950s. A number of factors have helped to mask this problem – until now.

Because rates of profit are relatively low there is less scope for investment in production. Instead, large pools of capital wash around the globe in search of more suitable outlets – ones which offer higher and/or faster returns. Overwhelmingly, this surplus derives from the substantial savings held by US corporations, from countries such as India and particularly China, whose economies have boomed in recent years, and from exporters of oil and other commodities whose prices are soaring.

This capital surplus, in its relentless search for swift returns, has served to fuel "bubbles" that disguise the underlying problems. "Bubbles always implode: by definition a bubble involves a non-sustainable pattern of price changes or cash flows".[194] These include the dotcom boom in the US stock market in the 1990s, property bubbles seen in many

---

[194] Kindleberger, C, Aliber, R, Manias, Panics and Crashes: A History of Financial Crisis (Great Britain: Palgrave Macmillan, 2005) pp 1.

countries in the past 20 years, and the subprime mortgage boom since 2002. In addition, this money also helps finance unprecedented levels of consumer debt in Britain, the US, and elsewhere.

Debt plays a crucial role in this paradigm. For the capitalist system to function its output must be consumed. If profit rates were as high as in the 1950s it would be a trivial matter for companies to invest their capital in new plant and expand production. But because profit rates have fallen, consumers have provided the necessary demand to keep the system moving forward, and – due to sustained downward pressure on wages – this consumption is largely paid for by debt. Broadly speaking, the general populations of all the western countries have been living beyond their means, and even now are being actively and aggressively encouraged to do so by the banks.

But it would be a mistake to describe the present situation as one of permanent crisis, rather it is one of recurrent economic crises. Sustained, low levels of profitability in the past do not stop capitalists imagining that there are miraculous profits to be made in the future and sucking in surplus value from all over the world to be ploughed into projects aimed at obtaining them. Many of these ventures are merely speculative gambles in spheres which are unproductive, as with bubbles in real estate, commodity markets, share prices and so on. But in the relentless and perpetual quest to expand, often with the help of financial innovation, capitalism also pours resources into potentially productive sectors, and so creates rapid booms which can span several years. Investment in the US doubled between 1991 and 1999.[195] When the bubble burst it was found that a massive investment in tangible assets such as fibre optic telecommunication networks had been undertaken that would never be profitable. While this period did see some real recovery in the rate of profit, that did not do away with the expectation that speculative profits could be sought where they did not really exist.

There are signs that the US, and perhaps also Britain, may be approaching a similar phase now.

---

[195] Leiva, OC. (2007) "The World Economy and the US at the Beginning of the 21st Century", Latin American Perspectives, vol. 134, no 1.

Investment in the US, after declining in the last recession, has now recovered to the levels of the late 1990s.[196] But the US recovery has been built on huge government deficits, on balance of payments deficits covered by heavy inflows of lending from abroad, and on consumer debt to cover their living costs –

U.S. personal income grew 6.2 percent in 2007, down from 6.7 percent in 2006, according to preliminary estimates released today by the U.S. Bureau of Economic Analysis.[197]

This is the background to the upsurge of speculative venture capitalism such as hedge funds, derivatives markets, the housing bubble and, now, massive borrowing for private equity takeovers of very large corporations. Against such a background,

---

[196] Leiva, OC. (2007) "The World Economy and the US at the Beginning of the 21st Century", Latin American Perspectives, vol. 134, no 1, pp 11.
[197]

http://www.bea.gov/newsreleases/regional/spi/spi_newsreleas e.htm

corporate profits[198] are being puffed up until they lose touch with reality, and just when things seem to be going very well, overnight it is discovered they are actually going very badly. And – as they say – when the US gets a cold, the UK can easily catch influenza.

It seems indisputable that the financial markets are, and have been for some time, out of control. The Capital Requirements Directive is nothing more than an attempt, no doubt a well-intentioned one, to impose such control via a legislative regime. However, it is also clear that there remains an irresolvable conflict between the proposed legislation on the one hand and economic and political considerations on the other. Given the complexity of the regulations; the difficulties entailed in applying them evenly across the European Community; the absence of any serious attempt to render the financial sector publicly accountable; and the enduring tendency of financiers to act in a manner

---

[198] Corporate profits provide the single best "bottom line" assessment of the current health and future prospects of the corporate sector: Himmelberg, CP, Mahoney, JM, Bang, A, Chernoff, B. (2004) "Recent Revisions to Corporate Profits: What We Know and When We Knew it", available at SSRN: http://papers.ssrn.com, accessed 8th April 2008.

divorced from reality, it is difficult to see how the Capital Requirements Directive will resolve the instability, difficulties, and tendency toward crisis which are inherent in the present financial system.

In conclusion: CRD will not resolve the present crisis and will fail to impose the discipline on the market as a whole which is so desperately needed. The exposure of large credit risks faced by the institutions will, arguably, be exacerbated by the regulations, and it seems likely that this in turn will trigger a downward spiral in the value of financial instruments.

Banks, financial institutions, regulators, accountants, lawyers, and governments continue to squabble over the clauses and terms contained within the CRD legislation and to tinker with its internal mechanisms. Meanwhile the world staggers on, blundering from one financial crisis to another while anxiously surveying the prospect of a cyclical descent into further war, social eruption, and barbarism. Put bluntly, CRD is akin to treating a gaping chest wound with a sticking plaster.

The banking system, esoteric though it may seem, is nevertheless a social activity and, like any such activity, it does not operate within a social vacuum. That said, it is difficult to envisage a change in the fundamental structure of the banking system without a corresponding change in the structure of society itself.

RESCUE PACKAGE [199]

---

[199] Ingram Pinn illustration available at http://search.ft.com, accessed 17th October 2008

BIBLIOGRAPHY

BOOKS

1. Craig, P, De Búrca, G, EU Law, Text, Cases, and Materials, fourth edition, (Oxford: Oxford University Press, 2008).

2. Davies, EP, Debt, Fragility and Systemic Risk (United States: Oxford University Press, 1992).

3. Goodhart, CAE, The Emerging Framework of Financial Regulation, (London: Central Banking Publication Ltd., 1998)

4. Holgate, P, Accounting for Lawyers (Cambridge: Cambridge University Press, 2006).

5. Langendijk, H, Swagerman, D, Verhoog, W, Is Fair Value Fair? (Chichester: John Wiley & Son Ltd, The Atrium, 2003).

6. Mishkin, F, Prudential Supervision: Why is it important and what are the issues? (Cambridge, US: National Bureau of Research, Inc., 2000).

7. Nesvetailova, A, Fragile Finance, (Basingstoke: Pelgrave Macmillan, 2007).

8. Mitchener, KJ, Are Prudential Supervision and Regulation Pillars of Financial Stability? (US, Cambridge: National Bureau of Economic Research, Inc., 2006).

9. Semyon, R, Measurement error and uncertainties: theory and practice, (New York: AIP Press, c2000).

JOURNALS

10. Accounting Standard Board. (2007) "ASB responds to IAS on Discussion Paper – 'Fair Value

Measurements"', available at http://lexisnexis.com/uk

11. Amery, P. (2008) "Too heavy financial regulation has created danger", Financial Times, at http://search.ft.com.

12. Arnold, M. (2008) "Fed just made matters worse, says Carlyle", Financial Times, available at http://search.ft.com.

13. Bank of England. (2007) "Turmoil in Financial Markets: What Can Central Banks Do?", at www.lexisnexis.com.uk.

14. Barry Eichengreen as cited in Atkins, R. (2008) "Heightened resistance? Eurozone 'decoupling' from US economy will be put to the test", Financial Times, at http://search.ft.com.

15. Barth and Landsman (1995) as cited in Bhat, G. (2008) "Risk Relevance of Fair Value Gains and Losses, and the Impact of Disclosure and Corporate Governance", Rotman School of Management, University of Toronto, available at http://ssrn.com.

16. Betts, P. (2007) "A history lesson in the wake of Northern Rock crisis", Financial Times, at http://search.ft.com.

17. Bhat, G. (2008) "Risk Relevance of Fair Value Gains and Losses, and the Impact of Disclosure and Corporate Governance", Rotman School of Management, University of Toronto, available at SSRN: http://ssrn.com.

18. Bollen, B. (2008) "Less risk, more kudos on the stock exchange", Financial Times, at http://search.ft.com.

19. Bouchaud, J, Gefen, Y, Potters, M, Wyart, M. (2003) "Fluctuations and response in financial markets: the subtle nature of 'random' price changes", at SSRN: http://papers.ssrn.com.

20. Chancellor, E. (2008) "A new-found respect for uncertainty", Financial Times, at http://search.ft.com.

21. Chen, K, Sommers, G, Taylor, G. (2006) "Fair Value's Affect on Accounting's Ability to Predict Future Cash Flows: A Glance Back and a Look at the

Potential Impact of Reaching the Goal", at SSRN: http://ssrn.com/abstract=930702.

22. Cienski, J. (2006) "Unified financial services supervisory agency", Financial Times, available at http://search.ft.com.

23. Davies, P. "Insight: True impact of market-to-market on the credit crisis", Financial Times, 2008, available at http://www.ft.com/home/uk.

24. Dizard, J. (2008) "Raising equity is top of to-do list", Financial Times at http://search.ft.com.

25. Dumenil, G, Lévy, D. (2001) "The Profit Rate: Where and How Much Did it Fall? Did It Recover? (USA 1948-1997)", Review of Radical Political Economics, at http://www.ingentaconnect.com.

26. Duyn, A, Wilson, J, (2008) "FGIC sues IKB over $1.9bn liabilities", Financial Times at http://www.ft.com/home/uk

27. Eichengreen, B, Mitchener, K. (2003) "The Great Depression as a credit boom gone wrong", Bank of International Settlements, available at SSRN: http://papers.ssrn.com

28. Financial Times. (2008) "Not yet time for a bail-out of banks", at http://search.ft.com.

29. Greenspan, A. (2008) "We will never have a perfect model of risk", Financial Times at http://search.ft.com.

30. Guha, K, (2008) "Banks take blame for credit crisis", Financial Times, available at http://www.ft.com/home/uk.

31. Guha, K. (2008) "Experts speculate on unorthodox policy measures", Financial Times, at http://search.ft.com.

32. Highes, J. (2008) "Concept of 'fair value' ignores stench of the real world", Financial Times, at http://www.ft.com/home/uk.

33. Himmelberg, CP, Mahoney, JM, Bang, A, Chernoff, B. (2004) "Recent Revisions to Corporate Profits: What We Know and When We Knew it", at http://papers.ssrn.com.

34. Hughes, J. (2008) "Companies face being forced to reveal off-balance sheet vehicles", Financial Times at http://search.ft.com.

35. Hughes, J., Goff, S. (2008) "FSA to admit mistakes in handling Rock", Financial Times, at http://search.ft.com.

36. Jopson, B. (2007) "UK Accountants hit out at 'fair value' rules", Financial Times, available at http://www.ft.com/home/uk.

37. Kindleberger, C, Aliber, R, Manias, Panics and Crashes: A History of Financial Crisis (Great Britain: Palgrave Macmillan, 2005) pp1.

38. Koo, R. (2008) "Insight: Japan's lessons could ease crisis", Financial Times, 2008, available at http://search.ft.com.

39. Larsen, P, Tait, N. (2008) "EU warning systems 'need strengthening'", Financial Times, at http://search.ft.com.

40. Leiva, OC. (2007) "The World Economy and the US at the Beginning of the 21st Century", Latin American Perspectives, vol. 134, no 1.

41. Mackenzie, M, Atkins, R. (2008) "Central banks act to calm financial markets", Financial Times, at http://search.ft.com.

42. Mackintosh, M. (2008) "Back to the roots with a high-risk hedge fund", Financial Times, available at http://search.ft.com.

43. Martin Wolf, M. (2008) "Going, going, gone: a rising auction of scary scenarios", Financial Times at http://search.ft.com.

44. Mayers, J. (2008) "Markets just could not self-correct", Financial Times, at http://search.ft.com.

45. Mitchell, L. (2006) "Convertible Bond that offers lifetime to some small companies", Financial Times, at http://search.ft.com.

46. Peasnell, K. (2006) "Institution-specific value", Monetary and Economic Department, No. 210.

47. Plender, J. (2008) "Financial crisis presents a test for fair value accounting", Financial Times, available at http://www.ft.com/home/uk.

48. Sevastopulo, D. (2008) "Fed cuts bank rate to boost confidence", Financial Times, available athttp://search.ft.com.

49. Soble, J, Full impact of squeeze 'has yet to be felt', 2008, Financial Times, at http://search.ft.com.

50. Staff team led by Enria, A. (2004) "Fair Value Accounting and Financial Stability", Ocassional Paper No.13.

51. Sullivan, R. (2007) "Regional Profit Rates of National Banks and the Development of the U.S. Financial Market, 1870-1914", Federal Reserve Bank of Kansas City, at SSRN: http://papers.ssrn.com.

52. The EU two years after the adoption of IFRS, Insight, Q4, 2007, p.4 at www.iasb.org

53. Tweedie, D. (2008) "Solutions now sought to add transparency", Financial Times.

54. Van Duyn, A, Guerrera, F, White, B. (2008) "Ambac shares lose almost a fifth over $1.5bn recapitalisation plan", Financial Times at http://search.ft.com.

55. Ward, J. (2002) "The Supervisory Approach: A critique", ESRC Centre for Business Research.

56. Whalen, C. (2008) "The Subprime Crisis - Cause, Effect and Consequences," at http://papers.ssrn.com.

57. Yorulmazer, T. (2008) "Liquidity, Bank Runs and Bailouts: Spillover Effects During the Northern Rock Episode 1", Federal Reserve Bank of New York at http://papers.ssrn.com accessed 25 March 2008.

DIRECTIVES

58. Directive 2006/48/EC of 14 June 2006 relating to the taking up and pursuit of the business of credit institutions.

59. Directive 2006/49/EC of 14 June 2006 on the capital adequacy of investment firms and credit institutions.

60. Directive 2004/39/EC of the European Parliament and of the Council of 21 April 2004 on markets in financial instruments.

61. Directive 86/635/EEC of 8 December 1986 on the annual accounts and consolidated accounts of banks and other financial institutions.

62. Directive 95/46/EC on the protection of individuals with regard to the processing of personal data and the free movement of such data.

63. Directive 2004/109/ECof 15 December 2004 on the harmonisation of transparency requirements in relation to information about issuers whose securities are admitted to trading on a regulated market and amending Directive 2001/34/EC.

64. Directive 2001/34/EC of 28 May 2001 on the admission of securities to official stock exchange listing and on information to be published on those securities.

65. Basel II: International Convergence of Capital Measurement and Capital Standards: A Revised Framework available at http://www.bis.org

STATUTES

66. The Finance Act 1998

CASES

67. Barings plc (In liquidation) & Anor v Coopers & Lybrand (A firm) & Ors: Barings Futures (Singapore) Pte Ltd (In liquidation) v Mattar & 36 Ors (2003).

68. Case 26-62 Van Gend en Loos [1963] ECR 13.

69. MGN Pension Trustees Ltd v Bank of America National Trust and Savings Association and another (Serious Fraud Office intervening); Bishopsgate Investment Management Ltd v Crédit Suisse (Serious Fraud Office intervening) [1995] 2 All ER 355.

70. Re Maxwell Communications Corporation plc, Homan v Vogel [1994] BCC 741.

71. Sphere Drake Insurance Ltd and another v Euro International Underwriting Ltd and others [2003] EWHC 1636.

OTHER SOURCES

72. 22070. IAS 39: Determination of fair value, Inland Revenue Manuals, 2005, at http://www.lexisnexis.com.

73. Basel II: International Convergence of Capital Measurement and Capital Standards, at http://www.bis.org.

74. IASB Discussion Paper (for comments only) and can be accessed at www.iasb.org.

75. Ingram Pinn illustration available at http://search.ft.com.

76. Landsman, W. (2006) "Fair value accounting for financial instruments: some implications for bank regulation", Monetary and Economic Department, available at http://www.bis.org/publ/work209.pdf.

77. The EU two years after the adoption of IFRS, Insight, Q4, 2007, p.4 at www.iasb.org.

78. The Institute of Chartered Accountants, Fair Value Accounting available at www.icaew.co.uk

OTHER WEB LINKS

79. http://www.maritimelondon.com/london_matte rs/18uly03_main.shtm

80. http://www.bea.gov/newsreleases/regional/spi/ spi_newsrelease.htm

www.ingramcontent.com/pod-product-compliance
Lightning Source LLC
Chambersburg PA
CBHW070409200326
41518CB00011B/2121